DELILAH CROWDER

THE
LAW OF
MANIFESTATION

ACCELERATING GOD'S PROMISES IN YOUR LIFE

DELILAH CROWDER

THE
LAW OF
MANIFESTATION

ACCELERATING GOD'S PROMISES IN YOUR LIFE

Published by
DPC Ministries International Inc.
All Rights Reserved

All scripture quotations were taken from the King James and New Kings James versions of the Bible.

ISBN-13:978-0-692-85002-2
ISBN-13:10-0692-85002-3

Editing by Silvana Freddi
Translation by Veronica Best
Design by Sergio Helguera

CONTENTS

INTRODUCTION

For the most part, the promises of God are bound to His plan and His purpose for our lives. These promises also come to us as desires of our heart. In Psalms 37:4, we read, "Delight yourself in the Lord, and He will give you the desires of your heart."

Delight yourself means to take pleasure in, find satisfaction, surround yourself, commit yourself, and trust in God. It has to do with searching His Word and submerging ourselves in His presence. Once we are there, immersed in His presence, where our will is totally surrendered to Him and our lives completely belong to Him, the Lord puts desires in our hearts that are aligned with His plan and His promises for us. These wonderful promises come directly from the heart of the Father and we can be sure that sooner or later, we will see them manifested in our lives. Why? Because they are perfect promises with a purpose.

This book has been written with the purpose of helping you see God's promises made manifest in your life. At one time or another, different pastors and ministers share with me that many people in their congregation have lost hope in God's divine promises for their lives because they don't obtain victory and do not see those great blessings manifested for them and their loved ones. Likewise, I have also been in the same situation where I have lost hope, and even though we don't doubt the power of God and His faithfulness, we reach the conclusion that such blessings can be manifested in others but not in us.

These individuals, who you may be able to relate to, hear sermons over and over again about supernatural breakthrough or the promise that is coming, but they never see it fulfilled in their lives. They pray, fast, read as many Christian books as they can, listen to CDs, watch DVDs....and still nothing new ever happens. The problem is not that God isn't faithful to His Word or there is some personal sin (although in some cases, it is), the problem lies in the lack of revelation and knowledge, and in many cases, a lack of application in our lives.

For many years I found myself in the same condition, full of frustration, and if I were totally honest I can say that many times I lost all hope. But thanks to the mercy of God, the help of the Holy Spirit and my perseverance, just like the widow in Luke 18, the Lord gave me revelation and the tools I needed to advance His promises to me. These tools have been my greatest help so that the promises I waited so long for could be made manifest in my life.

I want to share these tools and revelation with you in this book. I'm not only going to explain their Biblical parameters, but I'm going to go beyond and offer the clear and practical tools that you will be able to implement in your daily life and in your particular situation to begin to see God's divine promises made manifest in your life.

It's necessary to take into account that the promises and the blessings of God are made manifest in our lives as a result of revelation and understanding which are ministered to us by the Holy Spirit. In Genesis 12, God tells Abraham that He is going to make him great and powerful, and that He is going to bless him as a result of a revealed understanding (The Rhema Word). Later in chapter 13, we find ourselves with an Abraham that is now a rich man whose riches came as a result of putting into action the wisdom and understanding he gained from God. At the end of the chapter, God promises Abraham that He would give him everything his eyes could see, and what he could perceive by faith according to divine purpose. Everything came to life for this man as a result of understanding and revelation. You and I should seek this understanding and this revelation, and once we've received both, we should administer them to be able to manifest the promises of God in our lives. "Action" is precisely what many times is missing in our lives.

We read in 2 Corinthians 1:20 that "all of God's promises are yes, and in Him Amen, through us, for the glory of God." Note that it says through us. It is through you and I that these promises will manifest. Many people have obtained the revelation and understanding but fail in application. The structure and process we follow in our lives are what determine the type of results we are going to obtain. The Kingdom of God is manifested in us and through us. God's divine plan is that the world may see His blessing and manifested promises in our lives and in that way, His name of God is glorified.

Allow me to share a personal testimony with you. One day, during the summer of 2005, I woke up in the middle of the night with a question I had asked myself multiple times. Many of us have asked the Lord this same question a thousands times: "How much longer do I have to wait? When will I see your promise to me fulfilled?" Sound familiar?

For 17 years, I kept a promise to the Lord in my heart and waited for it to be fulfilled which, by the looks of it, hadn't manifested. I wasn't aware at the time that each detail of my life was getting me closer to seeing that promise manifested. It was that night that the Lord began to guide me and teach me a necessary process I needed to go through so that the promise I had waited so long for to be made manifest. It was just one of many pieces of the puzzle we call "God's plan."

It is possible that like me, you have received a promise from God that you have yet to see manifested. And just as it happened to me, you have felt frustrated, discouraged and even desperate on many occasions. Something I have learned from God is that, for the most part, He never tells us "when", "how", or "where."

This can be compared to when we make a purchase online and we receive an email notification that tells us the package will arrive in two to three weeks without providing any additional specifications. Then what do we do? Every day we look out of our window to see if the package has been left at the front door. Personally, I prefer to use an online tracking number that I can enter daily and know where my package is currently located.

Monday	5:00 am	Package has been registered/purchased
Monday	11:00 am	Jacksonville, Florida
Monday	9:00 pm	Atlanta, Georgia
Tuesday	5:00 am	Gainesville (ready for delivery)

Even though I don't live in the city of Gainesville, it is the center of distribution closest to my house; that is the reason why when I see that the package has arrived at the distribution center, I don't worry because I know that before noon, Peter, who has been our courier for many years, will be ringing my doorbell and with a wide grin, he will ask me for my signature and deliver my package and make a comment about the weather, among other things. How wonderful would it be if

God gave us a tracking number that we could use to verify the exact location of our promise?

Monday	5:00 am	Promise has been registered/given
Monday	11:00 am	Third heaven
Tuesday	9:00 am	Second heaven
Tuesday	5:00 pm	First heaven (ready for delivery)

Isn't it also exciting when the tracking number indicates that the package will arrive on Tuesday, but in reality, it arrives before its scheduled time?

In the book of Daniel chapter 10, we find the prophet receiving his package from the angel. This example allows us to know that there was a delay as a result of specific opposition that presented itself to the angel of the Lord. What a shame that Daniel didn't have a tracking number to know that his package would not arrive at its scheduled time. But just like Daniel, we can be assured that our promise is on its way and will arrive on God's scheduled time.

The angel said that on the first day Daniel set in his heart to humble himself in God's presence, the angel was released with the answer. Daniel did not stay home crying with his arms crossed; instead, he did his part in order to receive his promise. We can say that our relationship with God simulates a relationship in connection to our divine promises: He does His part and we do ours. If there is no cooperation or participation on our part, such promises will not manifest.

Remember that 2 Corinthians 1:20 tells us that "all of God's promises are yes, yes and amen, to the glory of God through us." All, not some, all divine promises, regardless of how large they are, how many they are, or how far they are, only manifest through us as a result of our revealed understanding taken to action.

In general, we always emphasize on the first part of this verse where we see, one more time, the faithfulness of God and it undoubtedly tells us, truly and assuredly, all of His promises will be fulfilled. But we forget the second ingredient or participant in this entire matter: us. In the following pages, we will analyze in great detail not just our responsibility in seeing God's promises manifest, but we will also learn the steps that we need to follow so that they are made into a reality and occur. I will share with you what you should do, day after day, in order to witness the manifestation of the promise.

We can compare it to a pregnant woman. Although she has only seen an image of her baby, not face to face, she prepares for nine months for the arrival of her child. She buys a crib, paints the nursery; she nourishes herself and exercises so her child will be healthy and strong. In the same way, we should prepare and establish the necessary means to see the promise that God made us, and have yet to see, be manifested.

In Genesis 6:17-18, we find God giving Noah a promise, "And behold, I Myself am bringing floodwaters on the earth, to destroy from under heaven all flesh in which is the breath of life; everything that is on the earth shall die. But I will establish My covenant with you; and you shall go into the ark—you, your sons, your wife, and your sons' wives with you." In the previous verses, we clearly see that God promises to save Noah and all of his family. Nevertheless, if we read verse 14, we see specific instructions that the Lord gave Noah so that His promise would manifest, "Make an ark using gofer wood." Once again, we see that in order for God's promises to be made manifest in our lives, there is something you and I must do.

That night in 2005, the Lord told me: "Rise up, dry your tears and I will show you." To Mary Magdalene, he said, "Why are you crying? Go tell them." It's time to rise up and put into action the plan God has made for our lives!

CHAPTER I

THE SECRET OF
THE ANCIENTS

*…who through faith subdued kingdoms, worked
righteousness, and obtained promises…*
Hebrews 11:33

We should give glory to God
because His children reached a great level
of faith. Many of them have experienced the
supernatural, have believed in the promises
of the Lord, and have warred for them in
the spiritual world. But, sadly as a lack of
understanding and administration, similar
to the people of Israel, many have also lost
such promises when they were at the point of

21

obtaining them.

We all know that a lack of faith, accompanied by fear, caused the Israelites not to see the promises of God manifested when they first faced the Promised Land. But I dare say that the mentality to attain everything easily also contributed to their result. Just like the Israelites, many people have confused the promises and blessings of God as something that is easy to obtain. Please, don't misunderstand me; I firmly believe that our Lord is pleased to bless His children, something that I have seen occur on many occasions, not only in my life but in others' lives as well. The point I want to make here is the same that I mentioned in the introduction: the divine blessings are manifested when we work in cooperation with God.

In Hebrews chapter 11, we find what many have created into a doctrine "The Hall of Faith." Here, we see men and women that reached the promise and walked out the blessing of God. The question we have to ask ourselves is, how did they attain the promises?

After reading about Abraham, Rahab and Gideon, we find in verse 33 truths revealed of how these men and women attained their promise: ...who through faith conquered kingdoms, performed acts of righteousness, and obtained promises... What did they do? First, they conquered kingdoms, second, they performed acts of righteousness, and lastly, obtained promises. These great men and women of the faith obtained their promise through a process, which required that they exercise their faith, conquer, administer and as a last resort applied justice. Each one of these steps were necessary so that they could obtain their promise. The problem lies in that we can easily do the first and second steps, which are to exercise faith and conquer, but we have so much to learn in reference to administration and application, because without those steps, we cannot see God's promises manifested in our lives.

BY FAITH

In Genesis 1:26, we read, "Then God said, Let Us make man in Our image, according to Our likeness; let them have dominion…;" later in Hebrews 2:7-8 it says, "And you set him over the works of your hands. You have put all things in subjection under his feet." God has given dominion and territory to men and women alike here on earth.

We can compare this to renting an apartment, where I am the owner but due to a contract, I give authority and legal right to another person or tenant to occupy that space. As long as the tenant fulfills the regulations listed in the contract, they will remain in authority of the apartment. If the air conditioning breaks, or the plumbing backs up, the tenant must communicate with me and give me permission to enter and repair what is broken. In the same manner, God has given us legal dominion of a specific territory, your house, your family, your career, your business, or your ministry. This spiritual law establishes parameters that govern both the natural and supernatural worlds. You and I have legal dominion here on earth, that is why we pray and we give spiritual authority to work on our benefit. For this reason, without a prayer of faith, we cannot see any manifestation. This prayer of faith is the method by which God can manifest Himself in the natural world and that is what we call "to be in agreement" here on earth with the supernatural. When our will unites with God's will, a connection occurs and the supernatural manifests in the natural.

The Apostle Paul writes in Romans 10:10, "For with the heart one believes unto righteousness, and with the mouth confession is made unto salvation." In other words, when we believe justice is manifested (we are translated, our position changes and we take action), our heart believes when we give legal authority to the supernatural. Secondly, we see here that with our mouth confession is made unto salvation (freedom). In the same way, everything we receive from God follows the same spiritual law that consists primarily in believing and then in confession, and it delegates legal authority over to the spiritual world so that the divine promises can be manifested in the natural world.

One example of this is when we receive

a Rhema Word, or revealed knowledge, through a message or study of prosperity. First, you believe you accept the Word in your heart; secondly, you confess it whether that is through word or works in tithes and offering, thus giving legal authority to God. Then salvation arrives. This is none other than how to be free from the financial stronghold that once bound you. That is why Proverbs 18:21 tell us, "The power of life and death are in the tongue." Everything we receive from the Lord works according to the same spiritual law of believing, confessing, and receiving. Everything flows from our heart; that is the connection we have to the Kingdom of Heaven. The problem emerges when the person cannot see what God sees; instead, they see poverty, sickness, failure, and they don't see themselves in triumph or as someone prosperous. God has empowered us with the ability to change what we see through our faith.

Now, let's return to Hebrews 11:33 where we see that things don't occur by simply believing alone.

CONQUERING

It says that by faith, they conquered kingdoms. Conquering speaks of working, imposing strength, and taking dominion. For you and I to conquer God's blessings and promises, we must acquire understanding of the subject or issue to be conquered, take power of it, and ultimately utilize that understanding for our benefit.

The author of Hebrews mentions Abel as one of the great men and women that conquered by faith, administered justice, and obtained the promise. Nevertheless, if we go to Genesis 4, we don't know in what moment Abel acquired knowledge of the necessary requirements for the sacrifice, but the fact that he found grace before God allows us to understand that he concerned himself enough to take the time necessary to acquire such knowledge. Furthermore, we find Noah acquired knowledge on how to construct the ark, and he applied that understanding which saved him and all of his family. In both cases, the first step after receiving the promise is acquiring knowledge.

God's blessings come to us through a Rhema Word, that is, revealed knowledge. In Hosea 4:6, we learn that a lack of knowledge brings destruction. In the book of Proverbs, we are exhorted, time and time again, to seek wisdom and to guard it like a treasure. In the Epistle of James chapter 1 verse 5, it exhorts us to ask God for wisdom, because He will give it to you in abundance and without reproach. This verse does not refer to spiritual wisdom alone but to wisdom in all aspects, administration and practical knowledge in our daily lives among other things.

Ultimately, you and I obtain God's promises when we acquire knowledge. If the received promise is in regards to health, it is our responsibility to study and examine all healing scriptures. But we can't stop there, we should search deeper and find out what science and nutritionists say in reference to our condition. Then we can make the necessary modifications in our daily diet and lifestyle. If the promise is in the area of business, it is necessary that we prepare ourselves by acquiring the best skill set in that field, we should study the market, find out what our client desires and who our competition is.

The problem with many people is that they remain seated waiting for God to do all of the work for them. The fault of such an attitude is ours and our leaders who constantly tell us, "The Lord is going to bless you," or "God is going to bring the blessing." And even though there is a great value of truth in what we say and teach, it is the individual responsibility of each person to fulfill their part of the bargain in their relationship with God. Remember what 2 Corinthians 1:20 says, "...all the promises of God are Yes, and in Him Amen, to the glory of God through us." In other words, God does His part when we do ours.

Abel and Noah not only obtained knowledge, but they also applied the knowledge and received something to their benefit. This takes us to the third point that we find in Hebrews 11:33.

ADMINISTERING

In Hebrews 11:33, we see that after they activated their faith and conquered, "worked righteousness." In another version, it says "administered righteousness." The terms work and administer speak of taking action. And action is what is missing many times in the people of God.

In Proverbs 13:4, we read, "The soul of a lazy man desires, and has nothing." May I ask you this question, What are you doing so that the promise of God may come to pass? Many may answer by saying, "Well, I'm praying, I'm fasting, I'm sowing, or I'm declaring." All of that is good and necessary, but what we do after prayer and fasting greatly influences and is a determining factor as to the manifestation of those divine promises.

To teach and be a blessing to God's people through these books is a promise I received from God and today, I can see it manifested in my life. Nonetheless, in order for you to have this book in your hands today, I did not only pray, fast, and declare the Word, but I also put my hands to work, I put my ideas in order, and then I sought revelation, inspiration and information. I also spent long hours in front of the computer, I had to acquire the legal rights and permission, and then I had to submit a manuscript to my editor and work with a graphic designer and after a myriad of proceedings, the book became a reality for you to be able to hold and enjoy today.

James 2:17 tells us that "faith without works is dead." If we look at Abel in Hebrews 11, we see that by faith, he offered a more excellent sacrifice than Cain. By faith, Noah prepared the ark. By faith, Abraham left from within his homeland and country. Each one of these Bible stories speaks of taking action after receiving a promise.

Again I repeat 2 Corinthians 1:20 where it says that "all of the promises of God are Yes, and in Him Amen, by the Glory of God through us." Possibly, what we are lacking in order for our promise to manifest is the working through us.

In Joshua 18:3, the leader challenges the

people that had entered the Promised Land with these words, "How long will you wait before you begin to take possession of the land that the Lord, the God of your ancestors has given you?" But Joshua did not stop there, because in the following verses, he gives specific instructions on what they should do:

The Plan

#1. Appoint three men from each tribe that I can send to explore the lands.

#2. Send them out to survey the land and to write a description of it, according to the inheritance of each.

#3. When they return, divide the land into seven parts.

#4. Judah is to remain in its territory on the south, and the tribes of Joseph in their territory on the north.

#5. After you have written descriptions of the seven parts of the land, bring them here to me.

#6. I will designate them.

As we can see, all of the promises that God made the people of Israel were made manifest when they, under the direction of Joshua, rose up and strategically took possession of it.

RIGHTEOUSNESS

The word righteousness may be defined in this situation as integrity and the ability to do things the right way. Something integral is something that is not altered or damaged. As children of God, we are called to walk in integrity of Spirit in each area of our lives. If we are not integral with our spouse, the promise of a happy home will not be manifested in our lives. If we deceive our clients, our business will not grow. If we are waiting for the promise of prosperity to manifest in our lives, but we are not integral with our finances and misrepresent our income or lie on our tax reports, we don't pay our creditors or we are poor stewardship, it will never be manifest in our lives.

A scripture that I repeat to myself, in times of confrontation or disagreement with another person, is in Matthew 26:22 where the disciples, after Jesus had announced that one of them was going to betray Him, asked, "Lord, is it I? Could I be the one Lord that is walking without integrity? Is it I Lord, the one that is behaving inappropriately?" In the past, even after I came to the Lord, I did things that lacked integrity. Actions that I am not proud of, but taught me a great lesson, that I have repented of and have been forgiven by the grace of God. That is why today I walk conscious of my actions, guarding my salvation with fear and trembling. Let's remember a little leaven leavens the whole lump. Also, certain actions we consider innocent and small can alter and delay the manifestation of our divine promises. What I'm discussing here, I did not find in a book and I was not told by another person; in actuality, I learned this information from my own personal experience and I can testify that as long as there is sin, lies and a lack of integrity in our lives, God's promises will not manifest. In retrospect, I can see that my lack of integrity—inability to do things correctly—obstructed and delayed my blessing. It is time that we judge ourselves so that we will not be judged.

In Joshua chapter 7, we see how the sin of Achan and his lack of integrity caused the people of Israel to be destroyed before their enemies, and they did not advance to take possession of the land God had promised them.

Let's learn from the ancients, from those taught about in Hebrews 11:33, "who through faith conquered kingdoms, administered justice, and gained what was promised."

ACHIEVING

Let's go back to Hebrews 11:33 where it tell us that patriarchs through faith conquered kingdoms, administered justice, and gained what was promised. Now can you clearly see the process?

Faith

Conquering

Administration

Righteousness

Each step was necessary in achieving what God had promised. In the same way, if you and I want to achieve the divine promises, we need to activate the spiritual laws. In my book The Law of Sowing and Reaping, I take the reader by the hand, step by step through the process of farming, the way each instrument works, and steps a farmer takes to teach us spiritual laws that are necessary so that the promises of financial prosperity can be manifested in our lives. The Word of God is replete with spiritual laws that should be fulfilled so that blessings may be manifested in our lives. You can't function in the United States by living under Mexican law and vice versa.

During one of our vacations in the city of Dubai, my husband and I were seated on the train headed to one of the malls when all of a sudden, an officer kindly asked us to get off the train. Once we were in the train station, we were escorted to a private area where the officer indicated that we were being fined $30 each for chewing gum, an act that is prohibited on the train. Even though there were no signs that indicated that chewing gum was prohibited (what my husband insisted to the officer and continued repeating for the remainder of our trip), apparently this fell under the category of food. My husband, very disgruntled as you can imagine, paid the fine and we now call that gum the most expensive chewing gum in the world!

As you can see, the fact that we weren't aware of the law did not release us from paying the fine. Likewise, in the spiritual world there are established laws that operate whether we are aware of them or not. You will not see your promise manifested if you don't apply the laws established by God. That is why in John 8:31-32, Jesus exhorts us, "If you remain in my Word, you are truly my disciples: you will know the truth and the truth will set you free." Keep in mind that Jesus was speaking to the Jews that had believed, believers like you and I. The Lord is telling us through the Apostle John, that the truth, the revealed understanding concerning a particular issue in our lives, will make us free. The revealed understanding varies from person to person and from situation to situation. Nevertheless, I would add that for that freedom to be totally manifested in our lives, we have to apply the knowledge we receive concerning that situation. In other words, "if there is no application of the revelation, there is no manifestation."

In the letter to the Hebrews, God left us with a map in which He indicates the steps to take to see the promise of God manifested in our lives. Until now, we've seen this map as if it were a satellite, from a distance, but in the following chapters, we will see it more closely. We will also reveal the spiritual and natural laws that bring manifestation to our blessing and promise.

CHAPTER II

THE LAW OF ADMINISTRATION

*…it is required, that those who have been given
an administration must prove faithful.*
1 Corinthians 4:2

Administration is the capacity that God gives us to be able to make decisions and follow a direction that will produce benefits in our lives. This includes the capacity to organize information, people, things, finances, etc. Through administration, we can observe and use details to solve problems and reach our goals or a determined vision. If you do a detailed study of the books of Numbers,

Leviticus, and Deuteronomy, you will find how the Lord is a God of order and pays great attention to details. Even in 1 Corinthians 14:40, we are exhorted to do everything in decency and in order.

During His earthly ministry, Jesus Christ administered and organized His ministry primarily through selected members of an intimate group of 3 disciples, 12 apostles and among them a treasurer; there were also another seventy disciples that were sent two by two before Him to promote His evangelistic crusades. The Word of God mentions in 1 Corinthians 12:28 that administration is a gift and even though we may not have the gift of administration or a title in that branch of work, we all have the ability to implant administration in our lives.

Without administration our lives and ministries and our business would be a true disaster. The church has been taught for many years that the blessings and promises of God will come suddenly and although there is certain truth in that concept, the fact is that without administration, there is no manifestation.

In Genesis chapter 41, we find the story of Joseph. There we see the administrative elements that were indispensable for the manifestation of God's promise in our lives. One point to consider is the meaning of Joseph's name "God saves." Also, Egypt is a type and shadow of the world while Joseph and the house of Jacob are a type and shadow of Jesus Christ and His plan of salvation for humanity. In this Bible story, Pharaoh had a dream and there was no one to interpret it, and until they called Joseph and as a result of the revelation of the Spirit, Joseph was able to interpret and bring forth instructions and an administrative plan presented to him by the direction of God Himself.

The Plan

#1. Therefore, Pharaoh should search out a man who is wise and competent to be in charge of all the land of Egypt.

#2. Moreover, Pharaoh should appoint inspectors in all of Egypt.

#3. During those seven years of prosperity, gather one fifth of all the harvest of the land.

#4. Under Pharaoh's rule, those appointed inspectors should store the grain of the good years for the time to come.

#5. Store the grain in the cities, so that there is plenty of nourishment.

#6. This stored nourishment will sustain Egypt for seven years of famine that will come and the people of the land will not perish.

Joseph was an administrator for Egypt and the neighboring regions including Jacob's house survived the famine, drought, and economic recession. Why? Because after they had received a word of revelation, the people submitted to Joseph who not only had a gift of wisdom and word of knowledge, but also a gift of administration. It was this gift of administration that put Joseph in a position of favor in the house of Potiphar and also his time spent in jail. We do not have to have the gifts of wisdom, word of knowledge and administration like Joseph in order to administer, but under the guidance of the

Holy Spirit and essential information and resources, we can administer what we already have in our hands, so that in this way, God's promises can be manifested in our lives. You and I cannot occupy what we can't administer. We can conquer it, but we will quickly lose it because we don't know how to administer. Someone can be the owner of the sower and have a great harvest, but if the owner does not administer wisely, he will not be able to enjoy the awaited results, much less its benefits.

In my book The Law of Sowing and Reaping, I dedicate an entire chapter to explaining how a sower after he has sown and cultivated a seed, administers the fruit so that he can enjoy the benefits of what he has sown. The majority of the people of God have a vast understanding of sowing and reaping, but nonetheless, they forget that they have to prepare the land, select the type of seed, care for the farming, gather and thresh the fruit, and do many other things before they can see His divine promise of prosperity manifested.

God can fulfill the promise of a husband and wife, but if there is no good administration, the blessing will be lost. If daily there is no love, respect, communication, and work as a team, the relationship will reach an end. You can reach the goal of owning your own business, but if you daily do not establish an administrative process, soon you will be closing the doors to your business.

THE PROCESS OF ADMINISTRATION

On this point, it is not my intention to burden anyone, or confuse anyone, asking themselves how to establish a strategic plan or an administrative plan. This strategic and administrative plan will be given to you by the Holy Spirit, in whatever way necessary so that the promise can be manifested in your life. Furthermore, the Word of God is full of instructions that in congruence with your personal decisions and particulars from the Holy Spirit and other acquired knowledge, you will be able to apply and obtain victory and see the manifestation of your promise or your blessing. What's important is you having an understanding that without administration, there is no manifestation.

In Isaiah 54:2, there is the "process of manifestation." In verse 1, we are exhorted like the woman who was told to rejoice even though she hadn't seen the blessing yet. In the same verse, this woman receives a prophecy as the first part of the promise but in verse 2, she is given specific indications which she has to follow in order to achieve the promise. These specific instructions are what I call the "process of manifestation" and I would like you to join me in studying in great detail this process in the following chapters. Once you learn this and begin to apply it in your daily life, you will witness dramatic and wonderful changes that will lead you to achieve the promises and blessings of God.

CHAPTER III

THE LAW OF DOMINION

Enlarge the place of your tent…
Isaiah 54:2

You and I have been created to be men and women that are more than conquerors, overcomers, and who realize daily that with the help of God, regardless of what may seem impossible, anything is possible. The Lord has empowered us to live lives of victory and blessing. Please, don't misunderstand me, I'm not saying you will never see adversity, but it is what we do during difficult times that determine if we will see the blessings and the promises of God manifested in our lives. Keep in mind that there can be no victory without a battle and no triumph without great effort. Throughout Scripture, we find clear instructions to achieving victory and these blessings. Unfortunately, we won't attain them if we don't take dominion of our territory.

In Isaiah 54:2, the first instruction that we receive is to enlarge the place of our tent. Your tent is your territory or dominion. When we speak of enlarging, we are referring to stretching ourselves, growing, developing in all areas of our lives, or in those specific areas that God is calling us into. The word enlarge can be defined as entering into deeper intimacy with God, acquiring more understanding of His Word, and rising to greater spiritual heights with Him.

Through the prophet Isaiah, God is calling us to enlarge our dominion. Dominion is that which is legally yours, the territory that God has put in your hands and that you have authority to maintain and control, whether in the spiritual or the natural. Your dominions include your house, your work, your business, your ministry, your emotions and your money, among other things. It is everything that in the present moment you can see, maintain, and possess.

The first thing we are called to do under the law of dominion is to stop, analyze and study. It exhorts us to make an inventory of our territory and dominion. Many times, we are so focused on the future, where we want to end up, and what we want to achieve that we find ourselves constantly running as if there was not enough time. In this way, we don't appreciate what we have in our hands and the season we are currently living in. Even though it's certain we should be visionaries and dreamers, at this time, God is calling us to take into account our territory and dominion. He desires that we enjoy our spouse, our children and our liberty to move without limits if you're single. He desires that we enjoy the small beginnings of our business and our ministry. He desires that we keep in mind that there is a season for everything, a time to try, a time to give up, a time to work and a time to judge. On a personal level, I am a visionary and I always have a project I'm working on, but thank God I have a husband who, although he is a hardworking and disciplined man, loves to have fun and clown around every once in awhile, which helps me maintain balance.

Before He can manifest His promises and blessings in our lives, God wants us to take total control of what is currently in our hands. The limits of our dominions can change and we have the capacity and the authority to do so, depending on the divine purpose for our lives and just how hard we are willing to work to see them through. Nevertheless, it's not guaranteed until we take control of what we have in our hands at the current moment so God can start to add more.

In Deuteronomy 7:22, we read, "The Lord God will drive out those nations before you, little by little. You will not be allowed to eliminate them all at once, or the wild animals will multiply around you." Little by little, the blessings come and we achieve victory and see the promises of God manifested in our lives.

CHANGE THE VISION

The second step in the law of dominion consists of having a clear vision of God's promise, our dreams, and our goals. Unfortunately, we can't dominate what we can't see. I would like to ask you, "What are you seeing?"

In Genesis 13:14-17, we read the following, "The LORD said to Abram after Lot had parted from him, 'Look around from where you are, to the north and south, to the east and west. All the land that you see I will give to you and your offspring forever. I will make your offspring like the dust of the earth, so that if anyone could count the dust, then your offspring could be counted. Go, walk through the length and breadth of the land, for I am giving it to you.'" In this passage, we see Abraham receiving the promise from God, a promise that is tied to its own capacity of vision.

Only you can determine the size of your blessing. And if you can see, you can receive, if you can see, then you can conquer. I ask again,

"What do you see? What is the size of your vision or your promise? Where do you want to end up? What would you like to achieve?"

If we look a little bit closer at these verses, they reveal two elements necessary to see God's promises manifested in our lives. In verse 14, it says, Look around from where you are; the first thing we should do is, see it. In the business world, the vision and the mission of a business are very important since they give perspective in regards to the surrounding world which is the purpose of the company; they also help the administrators and the employees stay focused on their principal goals. In the same way, when we have a clear vision of what we desire to attain, it is what provides direction. It's not simply about praying to God and asking Him to bless us. We need to be clear in what we ask for. The Epistle of James tells us in chapter 4 verse 3 that we ask and do not receive, because we ask incorrectly.

Returning to Genesis 13, in verse 17, we see that walking is the second step in establishing dominion. Go, walk through.

Even though God had made the promise, it was necessary that Abraham rise up and assume responsibility of his part in this transaction with God. You have to see it and walk through, and act upon it. Again, I ask, "What are you seeing?" Proverbs 29:18 says that without a vision, the people perish.

ENLARGE YOURSELF

In Isaiah 54:2, we receive instructions on how to enlarge the place of (our) tent, our territory or dominion. This is the third step in the law of dominion. We all have the ability to enlarge. Genesis 1:28 expresses it clearly, Be fruitful and multiply; fill the earth... But in order for us to be able to reach the next level of blessing, the first step to follow is to change what we are doing.

Without change, there is no advancement. Change comes when we analyze the actual situation and readjust its structure. If a businessman or business woman desires to see more productivity, the first thing he or she should do is analyze and readjust the structure. In the case of a home in crisis, the first thing that needs to be done is to stop and analyze the situation or the problem and then realize the changes necessary to improve the relationship. The problem possibly arises from the lack of communication between the couple or the quality of time they share together. In this case, both have to reach an agreement, guided by the Holy Spirit, with counseling and other resources. What you should keep in mind is that change, or the blessing, will not come from thin air. We have to take responsibility and do everything that pertains to our part.

Many women take years praying for their spouses and families, waiting for a breakthrough or that the blessings come to their lives, when God has already given them the solution. They have authority. Their homes and their marriages are part of their territory and dominion, they only need to take action and make changes in themselves first, and then in the situation. Every problem has a solution; God promises us that together with time, He will give us a way of escape. He will give you a way out, but you are the one that has to rise up and walk towards it. Do you remember what we spoke of in regards to relationship? You do your part and God will do His part.

Another type of person we will look at is the one who desires to see God's purpose in their lives and desires triumph to come to them all of a sudden, surprising them, as if it had fallen out of the sky. Even though God is all-powerful and can do miracles, this is not something we see in our daily lives. The purpose of the Lord is to have victorious children who are powerful, fully empowered and know how to exercise their authority without fear, and take control of their territories and dominions. He doesn't want spoiled children that receive everything they want without working for it.

At this point in the book, you may have realized that this is not as easy as some may say. The gospel of Jesus Christ, the promises and the blessings of God are for the valiant men and women who are willing to snatch the Kingdom of God, whatever it may cost. If you had the opportunity to speak with each one of the ministers, men or women, that have reached some level of ministerial victory, they will tell you that triumph costs hard work, effort, and perseverance.

God has given me the blessing and the privilege to do an evangelistic work to serve in His Kingdom establishing churches and ministries. Likewise, for over seven years, I worked as a ministerial consultant to over 250 churches and ministries and something I noticed was that the ministers who worked tirelessly, sacrificed themselves, and served in integrity moved forward and saw their ministries be blessed and grow. On the other hand, those that wanted to cut corners and take the easy route are nowhere to be found today.

We read in Matthew 7:20, "You will know them by their fruit." Our fruit shout to the four winds and tell of the level of intimacy we have with God. The fruit of our home, of our children, of our career and our ministries speak for themselves. And it is those same fruit that allow us to know if you are like the paralyzed man from Bethesda, who waited for someone else to pick him up and put him in the pool, or if you are like the woman with the issue of blood that proposed in her heart to put pressure on the crowd until she reached Jesus and was able to touch the hem of His garment.

Enlarging ourselves has to do with the use of strength and work and leaves behind marks that serve as signs of the sacrifices we have made to realize and achieve the blessings of God. A mother reminds her child in her time of discomfort and sacrifice that she went through the same thing, she makes mention of her stretch marks that testify to that truth. These marks took time to form and, for the majority of women, not all, are undesirable; unfortunately, they are part of the process and the blessing of being a mother.

Many people desire to grow and be multiplied and not suffer consequences. Behind every blessing, there lies a stretch mark.

CHAPTER IV

THE LAW OF CAPACITY

…extend the curtains of your tent wide, don't hold back…
Isaiah 54:2

I would like to start this chapter mentioning 2 Kings 4 where we find the widow of a prophet with grave financial problems. Her husband was dead and now her creditors demanded that she pay her debts, or in exchange, she would have to offer her children up as slaves. She went to see the prophet Elisha, and as soon as she explained her situation, he said, "Tell me what you have in your house." In other words, he was saying: "What are your resources?" He was referring to the law of capacity.

In Isaiah 54:2, it says that in order for a woman to see the manifest promise in her life, she must extend the curtains of her dwelling, that is to say she must add other elements to the process she is currently going through. In the chapter before, we are exhorted to enlarge ourselves, to administer what we have in our hands. Now we are called to extend ourselves, to go beyond what we have and prepare ourselves for a blessing. It says we should add to what we already have.

When a woman is pregnant, she prepares for the birth of her child by extending the curtains of the tent she lives in and she adds more curtains. Today, it would be like building an extra room in our house. She has to do this because the current capacity cannot support and serve the needs of the soon coming newest member in the family. In the same manner, we cannot administer new blessings and the promises of God under the same system or the same capacity that we are currently utilizing. In order to receive more, it is vital to extend ourselves.

During my years of apostolic work over one of the churches I established, I worked alongside a young minister and trained him to one day leave him in charge when the day came for me to open a new church. This young minister constantly complained that the work was too hard and that he couldn't handle the new members the Lord had recently saved up until that point. Nonetheless, on other occasions, he would say that he believed with all of his heart that God was going to fill every seat in that place with new converts. One day, without thinking, I asked him, "If you're complaining over the small things, how do you think God will give you much more?" And I ask you the same thing, "Do you have the capacity to receive the promise you have waited so long for? Have you extended yourself?"

Galatians 4:1 says, "As long as an heir is underage, he is no different from a slave, although he owns the whole estate." In other words, if we don't mature and grow spiritually, we can't take possession of our inheritance which is our divine promise. The Apostle John writes in his third epistle, chapter 1, "Beloved, I pray that you may prosper in all things and be in health, just as your soul prospers." This Bible verse clearly teaches that the level at which our soul prospers is the same level of prosperity for all other areas of our lives. We have to expand ourselves and grow in order to enjoy the blessings and promises of God and see them manifested in our lives.

It's natural to believe, which we generally do, that it's best to wait for the blessing or expansion to arrive and then we can make the necessary adjustments to enjoy and administer what we've received. But in the Kingdom of God, the process is totally different. If we compare 3 John 1:2 and Isaiah 54:2, we clearly see that the Lord desires us to be prepared before the blessing can flow.

In Isaiah 54:1-2, the prophet asks the widow to prepare before the blessing arrives. Take note that the woman is pregnant, even so God told her to arise and work, which lets us know there are no excuses for anyone. What do you think would happen if the pregnant woman had waited until she reached the hospital to buy a crib and prepare a nursery for the baby? My question to you is, "Are you preparing for the blessing?"

One occasion I was invited to preach to a church of about 100 members, and they could barely fit in the sanctuary, not counting the children and youth that met in another part of the building. At the end of the service, the pastor and his wife showed me all of the building's facilities. On our way back to the sanctuary, the pastor shared with me that he believed God would one day fulfill His promise to fill his church with 500 members. I immediately asked, "When will you begin the building expansion?" He responded, "When the time comes, we will see." And I thought as we say in the Caribbean, "Sure, we'll see…"

Let's go back to the widow in 2 Kings 4:1-7. Take note that the prophet gave her very specific instructions. In the first place, he told her to ask her neighbors for empty jars. She probably thought, "What? I don't have any oil, maybe you should perform the miracle first and then I'll go get empty jars," which is exactly what the majority of us think and do. We pray for the promise we have waited for, without having made any preparations. Imagine if he performed the miracle of oil without her having made preparations first. The oil from the original jar would start to overflow, then it would fall on the floor, she would start to scream hysterically, sending her children to run to the neighbors' houses and ask for empty jars. Meanwhile, the oil would continue to pour all over the kitchen and by the time her children return with the empty jars, it might have been too late to save any of the extra oil. In reality, the widow obeyed the prophet and prepared for the miracle by expanding her capacity, and adding more jars.

It's necessary to mention that when there were no more jars, the oil stopped multiplying. I ask myself, "What would've happened if she hadn't expanded her territory more?" Now I would like to ask you, "What would happen if you expanded yourself and prepared a place to receive your blessing?" It's sad to know that in the same way that we can extend ourselves, we can also detain the blessing. Remember, the oil did not stop until there were no more jars. God's blessing could have flowed much more, but it was the capacity of the widow that determined the level of that blessing. Even so, the Word tells us that the quantity of oil multiplied that day was enough for her to pay her creditors and live the rest of her life with her children.

PREPARATION

In Genesis chapter 12, we find God giving Abraham a promise which took much preparation and hundreds of years to be fulfilled. The Lord was giving this humble shepherd and his descendants a great region that was currently being occupied by nations like the Amalekites and Philistines. Just imagine if God had immediately given the land to Abraham, without preparing him to have the capacity for such a blessing. The inhabitants of those nations would've consumed him and immediately destroyed him. Abraham did not have the capacity to take possession of the land of Canaan. He needed to extend himself. That is why the Lord started a process of preparation and capacity. But many people are not willing to pay for that process and capacity. In those moments, many people give up and forget the divine promise.

In the book of Genesis, we can clearly see the process for preparation and capacity. We see the results that occurred to Joseph and Moses. In order for God to give the Promised Land to the Israelites, they had and to be empowered with knowledge, military strategies, construction, and government, among other things. They also needed the direction of a great leader that would guide them to take possession of the promise. Remember what we mentioned a few chapters ago, without administration, there is no manifestation. Now, let's add that without capacity, there is no administration and therefore, we will not see the manifestation of the divine promises.

That is why God prepared everything so that Joseph would end up in Pharaoh's Palace; that way, Jacob and his twelve patriarchs could travel to Egypt and after 400 years, his descendants would become enslaved. But in the midst of oppression, they were empowered to take possession and dominion of the Promised Land. In the same way, you and I go through certain circumstances in our lives that give us the capacity to enter into our own Promised Land.

The same occurred in Moses, as a result of being raised in Pharaoh's house and then spending 40 years in the desert, he received the preparation and capacity needed both in the spiritual and physical sense to be the leader of Israel. There is a common saying that says "there is no calling without a wilderness."

GET EMPOWERED

In order to see the manifestation of God's promises in our lives, we have to be empowered ourselves to possess and administer them. The process and the type of empowerment depends on the type of promise. If I am called to ministry, I should empower myself in the Word of God and in other areas that will prepare me for the ministry. The problem arises when we expect everything to be spoon fed to us like little birds. This mentality has contaminated a large part of the people of God and we have misinterpreted the laws of the Kingdom, believing that as kings and priests, we deserve everything to be given to us. In reality, there is some truth in this revelation, but we should not forget that we are subjects of a Kingdom, servants who serve a King. And in every Kingdom, there are ranks and titles according to the capacity of an individual. If we do not empower ourselves, we cannot govern.

CHAPTER V

THE LAW OF PRESSURE

...lengthen your cords...
Isaiah 54:2

The full manifestation of a promise comes just like any pregnancy, with birthing pains. In Isaiah 54, we are encouraged like the woman in this scripture to make all the necessary arrangements and to not forget to lengthen our chords and tie them properly by applying pressure. On the other hand, when the wind and storm comes, everything begins to be destroyed. We should be aware of the test, the opposition, and the adversity that will come to our lives and therefore, we must lengthen our chords properly in our home if we want to see God's promises become manifested.

PRESSURE

Human beings generally gravitate towards what Americans call their "comfort zone." It is the place where we are in neutral; there are no challenges, no advancement, and no development. Unfortunately, with every promotion and in all advancement, conflict will always come. Without conflict, there is no manifestation of the promise. In each situation, God desires to take us to a new level, He takes us out of our comfort zone.

Once an eaglet is taught to fly and search for his own food, the parent eagle will fill the nest with thorns so that when the eaglet tries to come back to his nest, he will be uncomfortable and get motivated to make his own brand new nest. That is how many of the conflicts that happen in our lives are not always an attack of the enemy. Sometimes, we have conflict in our occupation, or in other areas of life; other times, there are events permitted by God to take us to a place of blessing and manifestation of the promise.

In Genesis 50:20, we find Joseph after he had been sold as slave by his own brothers, falsely accused, saying, "You thought evil against me; but God meant it unto good, to bring to pass, as it is this day, to save many people." All of these occurrences brought him closer to his blessing and allowed God's promise to be manifested in his life.

The key to all victory is in this: Remain standing after any conflict. Conflict brings about change, and change births promotion. Once we arrive to the level God desires us to reach, we generally grow comfortable, but if we want to keep growing, we should allow Him to continue taking us through His process.

The prophet Isaiah encourages us in chapter 54:2 to prepare ourselves in moments of conflict through prayer, fasting, and greater understanding of the Word of the Lord. Any good soldier and great army prepares and trains himself/itself in times of peace and not in times of war. They establish defense tactics against any invasion. You and I cannot be any different. As we continue, we will analyze the strategic steps to follow in moments of conflict and anguish.

ALLOW YOURSELF TO CRY

In 1 Samuel 30, we find David living in the region of Ziklag where he makes an alliance with the Philistines, joining them and helping them fight their enemies. At one point, David leaves his camp unprotected to fight in the Philistine battle and in his absence; the Amalekites kidnap all of the women and children from his camp. This shows us that there are times when we fight battles that don't belong to us and put our own territory and dominion at risk.

After the atrocity occurred, David gathered his men and together, they cried until they had no strength left to cry. In moments of conflict and anguish, you and I should give ourselves permission to cry. Remember that

God gave us our emotions and they are not evil. It is what we do with our emotions in the midst of conflict that can become either something negative or positive.

STRENGTH IN GOD

After David finished crying, he rose up and strengthened himself in God. How exactly did he strengthen himself? He remembered all of the victories that the Lord had given him, and remembering the Lord's faithfulness. He expressed this strength in God saying, "I will lift my eyes towards the hills. Where does my help come from? My help (my rescue) comes from the Lord, the maker of heaven and earth." In Psalm 27:1, David says, "The Lord is my light and my salvation. Whom shall I fear? The Lord is my strength (place of security, refuge, rock) of my life; Of whom shall I be afraid?" You and I should take strength through the Word and the promises of God.

CONSULT GOD

In 1 Samuel 30:8, it says David sought

God's direction. He was searching for a solution to his situation. He did not give up. In moments of conflict, we generally feel confused and tend to make decisions we regret later. That is why, on those moments, we should stop and seek direction from God; when it is all said and done, He knows our beginning and our end.

In Hebrews 11:6, we read, "Without faith it is impossible to please God; for he who comes to God must believe that He is, and that He is a rewarder of those who diligently seek Him." When we seek the Lord, He responds and rewards us.

Jeremiah 33:3 is a very well-known verse that many of us know by heart: "Call to me and I will answer you." The word answer means "instruction or direction." God is saying through the prophet that in difficult times, we should call on Him and He will give us instruction and direction as to what steps we should follow in a particular situation.

James 1:5 is one of my favorite verses in the Word and has formed part of my daily prayer for over twenty years. As previously mentioned in chapter 1, James encourages us to ask for God's wisdom because He will give it in abundance and without reproach. The term wisdom that appears in James means instruction, direction, knowledge, understanding, discernment and revelation. This verse not only refers to spiritual wisdom but all types of wisdom, administration, and practical knowledge in our daily lives, among other things.

Through James, the Lord is calling us to search just like David in those crucial moments in our lives because that will determine if we see God's divine promises manifested in our lives.

PURSUE THEM

Continuing with the story of David in 1 Samuel 30:8, God gives David an answer as to what he should do. We read, "And God said, 'Pursue them, for you shall surely overtake them and without fail recover all.'" The words pursue them in this verse means to proceed, run, commit to a cause and pay attention to a situation. In other words, the Lord is telling us that in moments of conflict, we should not cross our arms or surrender, but it is a moment to be determined and continue in perseverance motivated by faith with the instructions that we have received from Him and take the promises He has given us.

In Psalms 18:37, David says, "I have pursued my enemies and overtaken them; neither did I turn back again till they were destroyed." This is the attitude we should take in moments of conflict: pursue our enemies, reach them and overtake them with the spiritual weapons God has given us. Remember also that it says in 2 Corinthians 10:4, "For the weapons of our warfare are not carnal but mighty in God for pulling down strongholds…"

We must "pursue" them, and then take action in that situation whether it be personal, ministerial, or professional. Pursue them! Do not hold back. Psalms 18:37 tells us that David pursued them until he overtook them and he did not return until every last enemy had been destroyed. David kept himself moving in the direction God gave him and until he saw a solution to his problem, he did not give up. In the same way, the Lord is calling us to persevere until we see the blessing in our hands.

CHAPTER VI

THE LAW OF MULTIPLICATION

…Be fruitful and multiply; fill the earth and subdue it,
and rule…
Genesis 1:28

One of the greatest and deepest revelations, but also overlooked revelation is in Genesis 1:28 where we read the first conversation God has with man when He tells him: Be fruitful and multiply; fill the earth and subdue it, and rule.

Don't you think we should pay close attention to the first conversation God has with mankind? In it, we discover God's primary purpose for creating humans. Genesis 1:28 is the map God wants us to use as we live our lives and experience the promises and blessings that He has for us. We were created and called with a purpose to administer or manage the earth for God, to establish and expand His Kingdom. Once He calls us, He also provides all the elements necessary to fulfill that purpose. The first thing we see is that He has empowered us with four very important and powerful elements that are found in Genesis 1:28.

These elements are to be fruitful, multiply, subdue, and rule. They are tools and skills that exist in each one of us and form part of life's makeup. If these elements are never utilized, they will offer no benefit to our lives; even though we carry them, we will not enjoy them. They are like applications or "apps" on a smartphone. What makes the difference isn't the box, but it is the applications, "apps" and the operating system. But what good is it if we have the best smartphone and yet we only use it to make phone calls when we could do so many other things like download our calendar, listen to music, read the Bible and even make our shopping lists and organize our lives in a way that is productive and practical?

These characteristics or revealed skills in Genesis 1:28 should be exercised in each area of our lives daily. As we utilize them, we will obtain more benefits and likewise, we will see the promises of God fulfilled in our lives. Let's look more closely at each one of these skills, or what I call the law of multiplication.

IT IS A PROCESS

Each element of the law of multiplication should operate in congruence with one another so that we may obtain the greatest benefit. We cannot put one into practice and leave the other. You can't be fruitful if you don't administer, and you can't multiply if you aren't fruitful.

We can compare it to a washing machine. It is a machine that has several stages in order for clothes to be fully washed: pre-wash or wash, spin cycle, rinse cycle, and then a spin cycle again. In like manner, the law of multiplication has a process established by God, of which we cannot alter if we want to see the full manifestation of His promises in our lives.

FRUITFUL

The first calling that God makes in Genesis 1:28 is to be fruitful, and even though many still believe the traditional church definition, when we read the Word in its original language, it speaks of being useful, to develop ourselves and to prosper in all areas. It means to take advantage of the elements that we have and the circumstances that we go through.

We are fruitful when we use what we currently have in our hands and at our disposition and make the greatest use of it. The first thing the prophet asked the widow in 2 Kings 4 was, What do you have in your house?

We are fruitful when we take care of the car we currently have while we wait on the promise of our new car.

We are fruitful when we work tirelessly as we wait for our promotion or our new job.

We are fruitful when we administer with excellence the salary we currently earn.

We are fruitful when we minister to the ten members of our church with love and excellence as we wait for the thousands God promised.

We are fruitful when we give our five clients the best service possible who will in turn recommend us to the next 500 clients.

In the parable of the ten talents, those who were fruitful with what had been given to them received the blessing in the end. To them, He said, "You have been faithful over a few things, I will make you ruler over many things." The law of multiplication consists of working little by little in order to attain much.

MULTIPLY

There is a law known as the "law of cause and effect." In other words, every action causes a reaction. This law also says that everything we concentrate on, will multiply. Once you concentrate on being fruitful in any area of your life, multiplication will undoubtedly come about. The problem arises when we concentrate so much on achieving what lies in the future that we don't enjoy or utilize the things we count on in the present. Remember what Matthew 6:34 says, "Therefore, do not worry about tomorrow, for tomorrow will worry about its own things. Sufficient for the day is its own trouble."

When we are fruitful, we take care of our children, we educate them, take time for them, and then have the satisfaction to see our work rewarded and multiplied when our children are recognized in their schools and communities. Also, we are fruitful when we see them go to college and fulfill their own dreams, develop their own talents and eventually marry and be good men and women.

The process is simple, fruitfulness produces multiplication. Do you want to be multiplied? Be fruitful. Do you want a spouse? Be fruitful while you are still single.

Do you want a great ministry? Be fruitful as a member of your church. Do you want your spouse to treat you better? Begin treating your spouse better. I don't know what the exact promise is that you are waiting to receive from God, but I can tell you from experience that if you begin to be fruitful in your present circumstances right now and wisely use your current resources, little by little, the Lord will add more to your life.

When did the widow of 2 Kings 3 begin to see multiplication in her life? She saw multiplication when she used the oil she had, she strategically administered and followed the prophet's directions. In the same way, when you and I follow the leading of the Holy Spirit in specific areas, we become fruitful and as such nothing and no one can detain the multiplication in our lives and the manifestation of the promises of God. I'll say it again, the process is simple: fruitfulness produces multiplication. As my pastor regularly says, "Use what you have, do what you can."

SUBDUE

One important part of the process of the law of multiplication is to submit or subdue the oppositions and difficulties that present themselves to us along the way. Sadly, the moment adversity arises, many let their hands fall and abandon everything, thus losing all of the manifestation of God's promises in their lives. What would anyone get surprised or feel as though they could die when tests or opposition arise? It's not that God hasn't warned us, He clearly stated this in Genesis 1:28 when He commanded us to subdue. In other words, He was saying, "Problems will come."

Jesus Himself warned us in John 16:33 that "in this world you will have trouble," and in Matthew 11:12, He said "the Kingdom of heaven suffers violence, and the violent take it by force." As they say in my country, "That's clearer than a rooster's crow."

The wonderful part is the second half of John 16:33, "He has overcome the world and has submitted all things under our feet."

To that I would add, "If He is for us, who can be against us? Greater is He that is in me than He who is in the world, which is why in Him, we are more than conquerors." If you and I want to obtain the promises that are kept for us, we have to confront and subdue all resistance that may rise up and divert us from reaching that place of abundance and multiplication that God has provided for His children.

RULE

The word rule comes from the Hebrew term: administer. And just as we defined it in chapter 2, administration is the capacity that God gives us to make decisions and follow a certain direction in our lives. This includes the capacity to organize information, people, things, finances, etc. Through administration, we can observe and use details to solve problems and reach our goals and our vision.

Allow me to remind you that without administration, there is no manifestation. And now, I will add that without administration, there is no multiplication. In Genesis 1:28, we see something very clearly. In other words, God says to man, "In order for you to enjoy all of the blessings I have for you, you need to follow the process I have established." Implementing and working this process gets us closer, little by little, to the manifestation of the promises of God. It is a simple process that constantly repeats.

To close this chapter, we can interpret Genesis 1:28 in the following way: "Administrate (rule) with wisdom (be fruitful) what you currently have in your hands, and with time, it will multiply; when opposition arises, confront it (subdue it) and you will see the manifestation of the promises of God in your life."

CHAPTER VII

PAYING ATTENTION

…lengthen your cords…
Isaiah 54:2

I Really like watching movies or series based on real life of great kings, emperors and conquerors and the way they achieved the impossible to conquer more territory. In the same way through the Scriptures, we can see the people of Israel as an example and a spiritual type and shadow of how we should conquer and expand our territory through wars and battles. In both examples, we learn that every one of the men and women were able to reach great conquests because they executed strategic plans and above all because they were very specific in their intentions.

During antiquity, people who lived in tents kept the fabric that formed their homes bound by chords which were stretched and fastened by stakes. The stronger the chords, the stronger the tent and the greater winds it could sustain. When there was a need for more space, longer chords were added to the tent's structure. However, many young families would include the longer chords in the original tent structure knowing that one day they would have to enlarge their tents for a growing family.

During our visit to the city of Olympus, Greece, the tour guide explained how in many regions of this country we were able to observe on the rooftops many bars or iron ready to build a second floor. Even though these bars did not look pleasing to the eye, this was a common continued custom as families prepared for future growth. We can see that the Greeks and those that lived in tents intentionally prepared for future growth.

There is an important element we must understand in order to see the manifestation of God's promises in our lives; you and I must act intentionally, aware of what we are doing, using our senses and abilities. The first benefit that we obtain when we act intentionally is that we have vision, a clear direction of where we want to end up and what we want to achieve.

The book of Proverbs chapter 29 verse 18 says, "Where there is no vision, the people perish." In other words, where there is no vision, people are destroyed; there is a lack of self-control, negligence, and a lack of direction. The majority of God's promises are manifested through a process that comes to us by revelation and instructions that He is giving us along the way. In Habakkuk 2:2, we read, "Write the vision, make it plain on tablets, that he may run who reads it." The Lord indicated to the prophet that he should write the vision so that whoever reads it might run with it. That is to say, when you receive a vision, you should study it, analyze it and put it into action so that it can reach its desired end. Because without application, there is no manifestation.

The second benefit of acting intentionally is that specific strategies are created, that is, technicalities and intentional activities destined to bring about the objective or vision that God has given us. Strategies develop into plans guided by the Holy Spirit or by knowledge we have obtained.

The third and last benefit of acting intentionally is the capacity to evaluate the process or the situation. Stop and look at the "pros" and the "cons" and act accordingly by restructuring and making the necessary changes. In the book of Ruth, we find two women who acted intentionally in the midst of difficult times and that decision allowed them to receive the blessings of God. We know the story of how Naomi returned to Israel with her daughter-in-law Ruth after both had lost their husbands. Once she was in Israel, Ruth began to work in the field that belonged to Boaz. She found favor with him who gave instructions to the sowers to allow wheat to fall so Ruth could gather it; this was part of the Levitical law where sowers were asked to allow scraps of wheat to fall for the poor to collect. When Ruth returned home, she told Naomi what happened that day and how she found favor in Boaz. Naomi used wisdom and gave Ruth instructions of what to do so both could be benefited. Since Boaz was a distant relative, they could apply the Levitical law of redemption in this situation.

Take note that Naomi's instructions were specific and had the intention of causing Boaz to redeem both women and marry Ruth: "Therefore wash yourself and anoint yourself, put on your best garment and go down to the threshing floor; but do not make yourself known to the man until he has finished eating and drinking. Then it shall be, when he lies down, that you shall notice the place where he lies; and you shall go in, uncover his feet, and lie down; and he will tell you what you should do" (Ruth 3:3-4). Finally, and thanks to the tenacity of Ruth and God's grace of course, both received their blessing. In Proverbs 16:4, it says that "The LORD hath made all things for a purpose," which means that He does all things with an intention.

In 1 Corinthians 9: 25-27, we read, "And every man that strives for the mastery is temperate in all things. Now they do it to obtain a corruptible crown; but we an incorruptible. I therefore so run, not as uncertainly; so fight I, not as one that beats the air: But I keep under my body, and bring it into subjection: lest that by any means, when I have preached to others, I myself should be a castaway." Here, the Apostle Paul tells us that an athlete takes action with intention by preparing himself, leaving behind everything that may harm him to win an incorruptible crown. He had his eyes fixed on the prize.

During our visit to Olympia, Greece, my husband and I had the privilege to visit the ruins where the first Olympic games were celebrated, and where the Apostle Paul took inspiration for those verses that we read earlier. The tour guide explained that the athletes exercised 364 days and did not take a day off or rest one single day; and they did all of that for a crown of leaves of ivy that would begin to wither within hours. Such athletes kept a strict routine of discipline and they intentionally prepared to be able to obtain the prize. Every believer should have the same goal as the Apostle Paul. Furthermore, we need to have other goals, other dreams, and other purposes. It doesn't matter the place or stage of life you may find yourself today, be assured that if you determine to act intentionally, you will be able to achieve all that you purpose to do. God is telling you today to lengthen your chords because your promise is coming!

CHAPTER VIII

PAYING ATTENTION

...strengthen your stakes...
Isaiah 54:2

Through the Word of God, He calls us to be diligent. If we learn to be diligent in every area, we will begin to live lives of more blessings and victories. We will be able to receive the divine promises for our lives. As we have commonly done in this book, we can define the word diligent as perseverance.

Perseverance means to be constant in what we have started; to position ourselves in a specific place permanently. I remember an old church hymn we frequently sang during youth camp meetings that said:

//I will give you the hidden treasures//

//Only persevere//

//Only persevere in the blessing that I gave you//

We have a seed, a blessing in our hands that exists to be cultivated and as a result, it will bring forth fruit, the manifestation of the promises of God. If we continue persevering, being consistent, the promise will arrive. The person who perseveres is constantly active, taking advantage of every situation, daily and little by little, getting closer to the blessing.

The author of 2 Peter 1:5 encourages us, "And beside this, giving all diligence, add to your faith virtue; and to virtue knowledge." It tells us that we should be diligent, that we should not leave for tomorrow what could be done today, especially if it has to do with instructions we've received from God and that will help us reach our dreams and His promises.

In Proverbs 12:27, we learn the following: "The slothful man roasts not that which he took in hunting: but the substance of a diligent man is precious." And it is here where many fail, in the effort and hard work they put forth. In recent years, a "generation of sustenance," or so I like to call it, has arisen. They are people who confuse the laws of the Kingdom with the right of sustenance; who desire to obtain all of the blessings of the Kingdom without commitment and without submitting to its laws. They are corrupt and irresponsible citizens. But the scripture says, "Be not deceived; God is not mocked: for whatsoever a man sows, that shall he also reap. For he that sows to his flesh shall of the flesh reap corruption; but he that sows to the Spirit shall of the Spirit reap life everlasting" (Galatians 6:7-8).

TALENTS

In Matthew 25, we find the parable of the talents that says, "For the kingdom of heaven is as a man travelling into a far country, who called his own servants, and delivered unto them his goods. And unto one he gave five talents, to another two, and to another one; to every man according to his ability." Our capacity is a crucial element in seeing the manifestation of the promise.

Matthew says that the man that received five talents and the man that received two talents were diligent and multiplied their talents, and extended their dominion. Nonetheless, the one who received one talent was lazy till the end and buried his only talent and lost his blessing. Being diligent consists of being wise in using the resources we have at our disposal, just like the man with five talents and the man with two talents. Diligence means being consistent and persistent in the administration of each area of our lives.

OBSTACLES

There are certain elements that can delay our ability to be diligent, and obstructing the manifestation of the promises of God for us. The first of these obstacles is fear—fear of the unknown, fear of failure, fear of the opinions of others. Every fear should be eliminated from our lives, first by recognizing it, then by searching for the root and finally by filling our hearts with the love of God.

In 1 John 4:18 it, says that "perfect love casts out fear." God's perfect love, His agape love that is described in 1 Corinthians 13 which says, "Love suffers long and is kind; love does not envy; love does not parade itself, is not puffed up; does not behave rudely, does not seek its own, is not provoked, thinks no evil; does not rejoice in iniquity, but rejoices in the truth; bears all things, believes all things, hopes all things, endures all things." When we receive a revelation of God's love for us, that revelation, that truth, casts out all fear and teaches us that the Lord has control over our lives and that everything works together for our good. Once we receive that revelation, we are converted into people who are diligent and persevering.

The second element that obstructs our ability to be diligent is discouragement. It mainly stems from a negative occurrence in our past or some lack of satisfaction in the present. We should be very careful not to fall into discouragement because our mood is the platform from which we face the circumstances of our life. In order to overcome discouragement, we should first admit our lack of satisfaction since we can't overcome it if we don't confront it. After we have admitted our lack of satisfaction, we need to analyze every area of our lives to prove which ones are producing that feeling, and then work on them until they are no longer a burden on our shoulders. Above all else, we should take all of our burdens to God.

In Matthew 11:28, Jesus said, "Come to Me, all you who labor and are heavy laden, and I will give you rest." The word labor in this verse means exhausted, worried, preoccupied, overworked and worn out with pain. If you have one of these characteristics in an area in your life, put it in God's hands so that He can give you a lighter burden and you can advance to being diligent in every area of life.

Ultimately, the lack of vision can obstruct your advancement and your progress towards the manifestation of God's promises. We have covered this topic extensively in chapter 3 where we explained that we can't dominate what we can't see. Where there is no vision, there is no manifestation.

CHAPTER IX

ACTIVATING GOD'S PLAN

…thoughts of good not evil…
Jeremiah 29:11

God has a perfect plan for our lives. In Jeremiah 29:11, it says that He has thoughts of good and not evil toward us. In this chapter, we see how to activate that perfect and divine plan. Because when God's plan is activated in our lives, the promises pertaining to that plan begin to manifest.

In most cases, God's plan is not activated because instead of seeking God's direction and His perfect will for us, we come to Him with our own agendas already designed that we present to Him so He will bless it and move according to our plan. And even though the Lord tells us in His Word to ask and you will receive, we should be aware that He is sovereign and has a plan that is perfect for us. He knows better than anyone as to what is in our best interest and what is best for us in each area of our lives. Remember that there are two types of will:

The perfect will of God

The permissive will of God

Many of us have lived the majority of our lives in the permissive will of God, not His perfect will, which always leaves us feeling unsatisfied. What do you want for your life: God's perfect will or God's permissive will?

There are certain steps to follow for God's plan to be active in our lives through our relationship with Him. Every relationship requires the participation of two people, as mentioned in recent chapters, God does His part and we do our part in order to see His promises manifested in our lives.

RECOGNIZE GOD'S SOVEREIGNTY

The first step in activating God's plan in our lives is to recognize that the Lord is sovereign.

In Joshua chapter 2 verse 11, we find Rahab the prostitute who activated God's plan in her life by recognizing God's sovereignty and became part of the Messianic bloodline. "I know the LORD your God, He is God in heaven above and on earth beneath" (Joshua 2:11).

Remember what we mentioned in the first chapter: everything we receive from God follows a spiritual law that primarily consists of believing, and then confessing, and as a result, we delegate legal authority. And that is exactly what Rahab did, she activated God's plan in her life. When you and I recognize the sovereignty of God in our lives, we let Him have control of everything. The plan He designed for us is activated day by day without delay, and we are closer to the manifestation that we waited for so long.

CHANGE OUR MENTALITY

The Word of God encourages us in Romans 12 to renew our thoughts continually. This renovation consists of substituting our carnal way of thinking with spiritual thoughts. As a result, we have the same mind as Christ. When this occurs, we stop living and making decisions that can distance us from God's plan and thus making way for the Lord's promises to manifest in our lives.

DECISION AND ACTION

Despite the fact that many people believe God is sovereign, they don't take any action in this respect. Even in James' letter in chapter 2 verse 19, it says that even the demons believe and tremble. The difference arises in our constant decision to take action and activate what we've believed and what we've confessed about God's plan. An example of someone who made a decision to take action can be found in Ruth 1:16 where Ruth exclaims, "Your people will be my people, and you God will be my God." Immediately, Ruth followed her mother-in-law Naomi to the land of Israel. Many times we receive God's revealed plan but our failure to take action causes that plan not to be activated in our lives.

TOTAL DEPENDENCE

In order for God's plan to be activated in our lives and see His promises manifested, we have to totally depend on Him to support our efforts and our human understanding. When David confronted the giant Goliath, he did not trust in own strength or previous experience; instead, he expressed, "You come to me with a sword, with a spear, and with a javelin. But I come to you in the name of the LORD of hosts" (1 Samuel 17:45).

In the Apostle Paul's epistle to the Philippians in chapter 4 verse 13, he wrote, "I can do all things through Christ who strengthens me." All of our dependency should be in Christ. If we want to see God's plan activated in our lives and His promises manifested in us, we must totally depend on Him in all areas of our lives where He has called us as parents, ministers, professionals and as business men and women.

PRIORITY

In Matthew 6:33, we read, "But seek first the kingdom of God and His righteousness, and all these things shall be added to you." In order to activate God's plan in our lives, we need to first work in His Kingdom and collaborate by expanding and establishing it wherever we go. When we make God's will and His Kingdom a priority in our lives, we activate His plan for us and He blesses us by fulfilling the dreams we have in our hearts.

In the book of Haggai 1, we read how the Lord sent a message to the people of Israel through the prophet. The message was simple and explained why the people had not seen prosperity in their lives.

The passage reads as follows: "Consider your ways! You have sown much, and bring in little; You eat, but do not have enough; You drink, but you are not filled with drink; You clothe yourselves, but no one is warm; And he who earns wages, Earns wages to put into a bag with holes." What was this all about? We find the answer in verse 9, "Why? says the LORD of hosts. Because of My house that is in ruins, while every one of you runs to his own house." The matters of the Kingdom were not a priority for the people of Israel and as we can see in the book of Haggai, as a result, they were not enjoying God's blessings in their lives.

In the same way, when you and I do not make God's Kingdom and His righteousness a priority in our lives, His divine plan is delayed and with it, the manifestation of His promises for our lives.

THE PROCESS

Each one of the elements mentioned in each chapter of this book is part of the process God has used and that I also use to make manifest His promises in my life.

Unfortunately, you and I are not the same, our past and present are different, and God's plan for you is different from His plan for my life. There may be similarities but in the end, the Lord has prepared a plan that is unique and exclusive for each one of us in which He exhorts us to seek Him with much prayer and fasting.

You may not be able to apply every single one of these elements in your life, but my fervent prayer is that you learn them and change your circumstances as much as possible, so that you can enjoy the Lord's plan for your life and the manifestation of all of the promises He has given you.

BIOGRAPHY

Doctor and author Author and Dr. Delilah Crowder is originally from Bayamon, Puerto Rico. Dr. Delilah came to the Lord as a teenager and has been preaching and teaching the Word of God for more than 30 years. She carries a PhD from Logos Divinity University and has also studies in Biblical Theology, Christian Counseling, Business Administration, Executive, Professional, Life and Ministry Coach.

Dr. Delilah moved to the United States in the 1990's, and throughout her evangelistic and missionary work has established 12 churches on the East Coast of the United

States. These churches have expanded throughout the Central and Western United States, Mexico and Central America.

In the last years, together with Asesor Ministerial Inc., a non-profit organization, she has contributed as a church and ministry consultant for hundreds of pastors, ministries and churches throughout the United States.

Dr. Delilah Crowder currently lives with her husband, Rev. Christopher Crowder in the Atlanta, Georgia area.

OTHER TITLES

Please contact us at

www.delilahcrowder.com

Made in the USA
Columbia, SC
14 October 2017